Volunteers to the Rescue

Monika Davies

People Help

Many people volunteer.
They help in lots of ways.
Some people might help keep parks nice.
Some people might help at food banks.

Jump into Fiction

Claire Helps

Hi, I am Claire.
I am a pilot.
I fly planes.
Watch me fly!

I am a volunteer too.
That means I help people.
I like to volunteer.
Watch me help!

Back to Nonfiction

Plenty to Do

Volunteers work hard.
They do good things.
They help people and animals in need.
They help for free.

He Helped

Benjamin Franklin lived long ago.
He invented many things.
He was a volunteer firefighter too.

Volunteers can be any age. Almost anyone can be a volunteer.

You Can Help!

You can pick up trash.
You can plant flowers too.

Helping at a Food Bank

Some people help at food banks.

They collect food.

They sort the food too.

Think and Talk

How can you volunteer where you live?

Food banks help many people.
The banks give free food.
People in need can eat.

Not Just Food

Food banks may give other items too. They might give things such as soap and shampoo.

People go to food banks for help.
Food banks help them through hard times.

Going Hungry

Many people do not have enough food to eat. Millions of people are helped each year through food banks.

Food banks give out healthy food.
This might be fruit in cans.
It might be beans or rice.

There are lots of food banks.
There are lots of volunteers there too.
They want to give their time to help.

How Many?

There are more than 200 food banks in the United States.

Good to Give

We all need help at times.
We all can find ways to help others.
Volunteering is one way to help.
It is a good way to give to others.

Think and Talk

How have you helped others?

Civics in Action

You can help your community. Help a food bank by collecting food. Here is how.

1. Write a letter to your family and friends. Ask them to donate food for a food bank. Be sure to tell them what type of food you need.

2. Gather the food they donate. Put it in bags and boxes.

3. Drop off the food at a food bank near you. A grown-up can help you!